Northfield Poems

NORTHFIELD POEMS

A. R. Ammons

Cornell University Press

ITHACA, NEW YORK

CORNELL UNIVERSITY PRESS

First published 1966

Library of Congress Catalog Card Number: 66-20500

PRINTED IN THE UNITED STATES OF AMERICA
BY THE SCIENCE PRESS, INC.
BOUND BY VAIL-BALLOU PRESS, INC.

to Blanche and W. M. Ammons

ACKNOWLEDGMENTS

Grateful acknowledgment is made to the editors of the following publications for permission to reprint the poems listed:

Accent, for "A Symmetry of Thought" and "The Wind Coming Down From"; *Carleton Miscellany,* for "Uh, Philosophy" (formerly "Canto 44"); *Chelsea,* for "One:Many," "Sphere," and "Two Motions"; *Damascus Road,* for "Discoverer"; *Hudson Review,* for "Contingency," "Interference," "Interval" (formerly "Poem"), "Reflective," "Sitting Down, Looking Up," "Unbroken," and "Way to Go"; *Kayak,* for "The Foot-Washing"; *The New York Times,* for "Recovery" and "Trap."

Niobe, for "Consignee"; *Poetry,* for "Composing," "Halfway," "Ithaca, N.Y.," "Joshua Tree," and "Landscape with Figures"; *Poetry Northwest,* for "Muse"; *Quarterly Review of Literature,* for "Fall," "Holding On," and "The Constant"; *Red Clay Reader,* for "First Carolina Said-Song" and "Second Carolina Said-Song"; *Tri-Quarterly,* for "Saliences"; *The Trojan Horse,* for "Height" and "Kind."

"Belief" first appeared in *Of Poetry and Power,* edited by Erwin A. Glikes and Paul Schwaber, published by Basic Books, Inc., in 1964.

"Passage," "Peak," "Self-Portrait," and "Zone" first appeared in *Modern Occasions,* edited by Philip Rahv, © 1966 by Farrar, Straus and Giroux, Inc.

The poems "Recovery" and "Trap" © 1964 and 1965 respectively by the New York Times Company. Reprinted by permission.

CONTENTS

Northfield Poems

KIND

I can't understand it
  said the giant redwood
    I have attained height and distant view,
    am easy with time,

    and yet you search the
    wood's edge
for weeds
that find half-dark room in margins
    of stone
    and are
as everybody knows
    here and gone in a season

    O redwood I said in this matter
I may not be able to argue from reason
but preference sends me stooping
seeking
    the least,
    as finished as you
    and with a flower

HEIGHT

There was a hill once wanted
to become a mountain
   and
forces underground helped it
   lift itself
   into broad view
and noticeable height:

but the green hills around and even
some passable mountains,
   diminished by white,
wanted it down
so the mountain, alone, found
   grandeur taxing and
   turned and turned
to try to be concealed:

oh but after the rock is
massive and high . . . !
   how many centuries of rain and
ice, avalanche
and shedding shale
   before the dull mound
can yield to grass!

JOSHUA TREE

The wind
rounding the gap
found me there
weeping under a
Joshua Tree
and Oh I said
I am mortal all right
and cannot live,
by roads
stopping to wait
for no one coming,
moving on
to dust
and burned weeds,
having no liturgy,
no pilgrim
from my throat
singing news of joy,
no dome, alabaster wall,
no eternal city:
the wind said
Wayfaring and wandering
is not for mortals
who should raise
the cock
that cries their
dawns in and
cannot always be coming to
unbroken country:
settle here
by this Joshua Tree
and make a well:

3

unlike wind
that dies and
never dies I said
I must go on
consigned to
form that will not
let me loose
except to death
till some
syllable's rain
anoints my tongue
and makes it sing
to strangers:
if it does not rain
find me wasted by roads:
enter angling through
my cage
and let my ribs
sing me out.

REFLECTIVE

I found a
weed
that had a

mirror in it
and that
mirror

looked in at
a mirror
in

me that
had a
weed in it

LANDSCAPE WITH FIGURES

When I go back of my head
    down the cervical well, roots
      branch
thinning, figuring
    into flesh
and flesh
glimmers with man-old fires
and ghosts
hollowing up into mind
      cry from ancient narrowing
      needle-like caves:

a depth of contact there you'd
      think would hold, the last
      nerve-hair
feeding direct from
    meat's indivisible stuff:
but what we ride on makes us ride
and rootless mind
in a thundering rove
establishes, disposes:
      rocks and clouds
      take their places:

or if place shifts by a sudden breaking
    in of stars
      and mind whirls
where to go
    then like a rabbit it
freezes in grass, order
as rock or star, to let whatever can, come,

pass, pass over : somewhere another human
figure moves or rests, concern
     for (or fear of) whom
          will start and keep us.

THE CONSTANT

When leaving the primrose, bayberry dunes, seaward
I discovered the universe this morning,
   I was in no
mood
for wonder,
  the naked mass of so much miracle
already beyond the vision
of my grasp:

along a rise of beach, a hundred feet from the surf,
a row of clam shells
  four to ten feet wide
  lay sinuous as far as sight:

in one shell—though in the abundance
   there were others like it—upturned,
four or five inches across the wing,
a lake
three to four inches long and two inches wide,
all dimensions rounded,
  indescribable in curve:

and on the lake a turning galaxy, a film of sand,
coordinated, nearly circular (no real perfections),
  an inch in diameter, turning:
turning:
counterclockwise, the wind hardly perceptible from
  11 o'clock
   with noon at sea:
   the galaxy rotating,
   but also,
at a distance from the shell lip,
revolving

8

round and round the shell:

     a gull's toe could spill the universe:
two more hours of sun could dry it up: .
a higher wind could rock it out:

the tide will rise, engulf it, wash it loose:
utterly:

the terns, their
    young somewhere hidden in clumps of grass or weed,
were diving *sshik sshik* at me,
       then pealing upward for a new round and dive:

I have had too much of this inexhaustible miracle:
miracle, this massive, drab constant of experience.

CONTINGENCY

Water from the sprinkler
collects
in street-edge gravel and

makes rocky pools : birds
materialize—puff, bathe
and drink : a green-black

grackle lopes, listing,
across the hot street, pecks
a starling, and drinks : a

robin rears misty with
exultation : twittering comes
in bunches of starts and

flights : shadows pour
across cement and lawn : a
turn of the faucet
dries every motion up.

ONE:MANY

To maintain balance
between one and many by
    keeping in operation both one and many:
    fear a too great consistency, an arbitrary
imposition
    from the abstract *one*
    expressed
    downwardly into the realities of manyness:
  this makes unity
not deriving from the balance of manyness
but by destruction of diversity:
    it is unity
        unavailable to change,
cut off from the reordering possibilities of
    variety:

        when I tried to summarize
        a moment's events
along the creek shore this afternoon,
the tide gathering momentum outwardly,
terns
hovering
dropping to spear shallow water,
    the minnows
in a band
wavering between depth and shallows,
the sand hissing
into new images,
        the grass at its sound and symmetry,
        scoring
        semicircles of wind
    into sand,

the tan beetle in a footprint dead,
flickering to
    gusts of wind,
        the bloodsucking flies
        at their song and savage whirl,
when I tried to think by what
millions of grains of events
    the tidal creek had altered course,
        when I considered alone
a record
of the waves on the running blue creek,
    I was released into a power beyond my easy failures:

not unity by the winnowing out of difference,
not unity thin and substanceless as abstraction,
    uneventful as theory:

I think of California's towns and ranges,
    deserts and oil fields;
and of Maine's
    unpainted seahouses
    way out on the tips of fingerlands,
lobster traps and pots,
freshwater lakes; of Chicago,
    hung like an eggsac on the leaf of Lake
Michigan, with
its
Art Museum, Prudential Building, Knickerbocker Hotel
(where Cummings stayed);
of North Carolina's
    sounds, banks, and shoals,
    telephone wire loads of swallows,
of Columbus County
        where fresh-dug peanuts
        are boiled

in iron pots, salt filtering
in through the boiled-clean shells (a delicacy
true
as artichokes or Jersey
asparagus): and on through villages,
along dirt roads, ditchbanks, by gravel pits and on
      to the homes,
inventions, longings: the small-business
man in
      Kansas City declares an extra dividend
and his daughter
      who teaches school in Duquesne
buys a Volkswagen, a second car for the family:
out of many, one:
from variety an overriding unity, the expression of
variety:

no book of laws, short of unattainable reality itself,
can anticipate every event:
      only the book of laws founded
     against itself,
founded on freedom of each event to occur as itself,
lasts into the inevitable balance events will take.

HALFWAY

This October
rain
comes after fall

summer and
drought
and is

a still rain:
it takes leaves
straight

down: the
birches stand
in

pools of them-
selves, the yellow
fallen

leaves reflecting
those on
the tree that
mirror the ground.

INTERFERENCE

A whirlwind in the fields
lifts sand
into its motions
to show, tight, small,
the way it walks
through a summer day:

better take time to watch
the sand-shadow mist —
since every
grain of sand
is being counted by the sun.

SALIENCES

Consistencies rise
and ride
the mind down
hard routes
    walled
with no outlet and so
to open a variable geography,
    proliferate
possibility, here
is this dune fest
    releasing,
mind feeding out,
gathering clusters,
fields of order in disorder,
where choice
can make beginnings,
    turns,
    reversals,
where straight line
and air-hard thought
can meet
unarranged disorder,
    dissolve
before the one event that
creates present time
in the multi-variable
    scope:
a variable of wind
among the dunes,
making variables
of position and direction and sound
of every reed leaf

and bloom,
running streams of sand,
winding, rising, at a depression
falling out into deltas,
weathering shells with blast,
striking hiss into clumps of grass,
against bayberry leaves,
      lifting
the spider from footing to footing
hard across the dry even crust
toward the surf:
wind, a variable, soft wind, hard
steady wind, wind
shaped and kept in the
bent of trees,
the prevailing dipping seaward
of reeds,
the kept and erased sandcrab trails:
wind, the variable to the gull's flight,
how and where he drops the clam
and the way he heads in, running to loft:
wind, from the sea, high surf
and cool weather;
from the land, a lessened breakage
and the land's heat:
wind alone as a variable,
as a factor in millions of events,
leaves no two moments
on the dunes the same:
      keep
free to these events,
bend to these
changing weathers:
multiple as sand, events of sense

alter old dunes
of mind,
release new channels of flow,
free materials
to new forms:
wind alone as a variable
takes this neck of dunes
out of calculation's reach:
come out of the hard
routes and ruts,
pour over the walls
of previous assessments: turn to
the open,
the unexpected, to new saliences of feature.

*

The reassurance is
that through change
continuities sinuously work,
cause and effect
        without alarm,
gradual shadings out or in,
motions that full
        with time
do not surprise, no
abrupt leap or burst: possibility,
with meaningful development
of circumstance:

when I went back to the dunes today,
        saliences,
congruent to memory,
spread firmingly across my sight:
the narrow white path

rose and dropped over
grassy rises toward the sea :
sheets of reeds,
tasseling now near fall,
filled the hollows
with shapes of ponds or lakes :
bayberry, darker, made wandering
chains of clumps, sometimes pouring
into heads, like stopped water :
    much seemed
constant, to be looked
forward to, expected :
from the top of a dune rise,
look of ocean salience : in
    the hollow,
where a runlet
    makes in
at full tide and fills a bowl,
extravagance of pink periwinkle
along the grassy edge,
and a blue, bunchy weed, deep blue,
deep into the mind the dark blue
    constant :
minnows left high in the tide-deserted pocket,
    fiddler crabs
bringing up gray pellets of drying sand,
disappearing from air's faster events
at any close approach :
certain things and habits
    recognizable as
having lasted through the night :
though what change in
a day's doing !
desertions of swallows

that yesterday
ravaged air, bush, reed, attention
in gatherings wide as this neck of dunes:
now, not a sound
or shadow, no trace of memory, no remnant
    explanation:
summations of permanence!
where not a single single thing endures,
the overall reassures,
deaths and flights,
shifts and sudden assaults claiming
limited orders,
the separate particles:
earth brings to grief
much in an hour that sang, leaped, swirled,
yet keeps a round
    quiet turning,
beyond loss or gain,
beyond concern for the separate reach.

TRAP

White, flipping
butterfly,
paperweight,

flutters by and
over shrubs,
meets a binary

mate and they
spin, two orbits
of an

invisible center;
rise
over the roof

and caught on
currents
rise higher

than trees and
higher and up
out of sight,

swifter in
ascent than they
can fly or fall.

THE FOOT-WASHING

Now you have come,
the roads
humbling your feet with dust:

I ask you to
sit by this
spring:

I will wash your feet
with springwater
and silver care:

I lift leaking handbowls
to your ankles:
O ablutions!

Who are you
sir
who are my brother?

I dry your feet
with sweetgum
and mint leaves:

the odor of your feet
is newly earthen,
honeysuckled:

bloodwork in blue
raisures over the white
skinny anklebone:

if I have wronged you
cleanse me with the falling
water of forgiveness.

And woman, your flat feet
yellow, gray with dust,
your orphaned udders flat,

lift your dress
up to your knees
and I will wash your feet:

feel the serenity
cool as cool springwater
and hard to find:

if I have failed to know
the grief in your gone time,
forgive me wakened now.

RECOVERY

All afternoon
the tree shadows, accelerating,
lengthened
till
sunset
shot them black into infinity :
next morning
darkness
returned from the other
infinity and the
shadows caught ground
and through the morning, slowing,
hardened into noon.

TWO MOTIONS

It is not enough to be willing to come out of the dark
    and stand in the light,
all hidden things brought into sight, the damp
  black spaces,
where fear, arms over its head, trembles into blindness,
    invaded by truth-seeking light:
it is not enough to desire radiance, to be struck by
  radiance: external light
throws darkness behind its brilliance, the division
    nearly half and half:
it is only enough when the inner light
  kindles to a source, radiates from its sphere to all
points outwardly: then, though
    surrounding things are half and half with
light and darkness, all that is visible from the source
  is light:
it is not enough to wish to cast light: as much
    darkness as light is made that way: it is only
enough to touch the inner light of each surrounding thing
  and hope it will itself be stirred to radiance,
eliminating the shadows that all lights give it
    and realizing its own full sphere:
it is only enough to radiate the sufficient light
  within that men for a long time have told about, the
constant source, the light beyond all possibility of night.

    However,

        in separating light from darkness
        have we cast into death:
        in attaining the luminous,
made, capable self,
        have we brought error

to perfection:
  in naming have we divided what
      unnaming will not undivide:

  in coming so far,
synthesizing, enlarging, incorporating, completing
(all the way to a finished Fragment)
      have we foundered into arrival:

  in tarring, calking, timbering,
      have we kept our ship afloat
          only to satisfy all destinations
by no departures;
          only to abandon helm,
sailcloth, hemp, spar;
          only to turn charts
to weather, compass to salt, sextant
    to sea:

as far as words will let us go, we have
      voyaged: now
we disperse the ruin of our gains
to do a different kind of going
that will
become less and
less
voyaging

    as arrival approaches nowhere-everywhere
    in gain of nothing-everything.

COMPOSING

An orchestration of events,
memories,
intellections, wounds,
hard throats :
a clustering of years into phrases,
motifs, a

keying to somber D-flat
or brilliant A :
an emergence
of minor meanings,
the loft of flutes, oboes, bassoons :
percussion,
the critical cymbal

crashing grief out
or like a peacock's tail
unfolding into spirit :
the derelict breakage of days, weeks,
hours, reorganizing,
orienting to the riding movement,

hawklike,
but keener in wings,
in shadow deeper :
a swerving into the underside
gathering
dream images,
the hidden flight of red-black cries,

darkness,
the ghosts re-rising,
the eyeless, furious,
mangled ones :

then two motions like cliffs
opposing, the orchestration at
first

too torn, but going back
finding new lights to doom
dark resurrections
till the large curve of meaning
stands apart
like a moon cusp or horn
singing with a higher soundless sound.

ITHACA, N.Y.

When the storm passed,
we listened to rain-leavings,
individual drops in

fields of surprise;
a drop here
in a puddle;

the clear-cracking
drop
against a naked root;

by the window,
the muffled, elm-leaf drop,
reorganizing at the tip,

dropping in another
event to the ground:
we listened and

liveliness broke
out at a thousand quiet
points.

CONSIGNEE

I have been brought out of day,
out of the full dawn led away;
    from the platform of noon
I have descended.

To death, the diffuse one
going beside me, I said,
    You have brought me out of day
and he said
No longer like the fields of earth
may you go in and out.

I quarreled and devised a while
    but went on
having sensed a nice dominion in the air,
the black so round and deep.

FEBRUARY BEACH

Underneath, the dunes
      are solid,
                  frozen with rain
            the sand
held and let
go deep
without losing

            till a clearing freeze
left water the keeper of sand:

warm days since
have intervened,
softened

                  the surface,
evaporated
the thaw
            and let grains loose: now

the white grains drift against the dunes
and ripple as if in summer,
hiding the hard deep marriage
            of sand and ice:

fog lay thick here
most of the morning
            but now lifting, rides
in low from the sea,
            filters inland through the dunes
but
                  over the warm and
sunny sand rising

loses its shape out of sight:

the dense clumps of grass, bent
                    over,
still wet with fog,
                    drop
        dark buttons of held fog on thin dry sand,
separately, here, there, large drops,
another rainsand shape:

distant, the ocean's breakers
merge into high splintering
            sound,
the wind low, even, inland, wet,
a perfect carriage
            for resolved, continuous striving:

            not the deep breakage and roar
        of collapsing hollows:
        sound that creation may not be complete,
that the land may not have been
given
permanently,
            that something remains
to be agreed on,
a lofty burn of sound, a clamoring and
            coming on:

how will the mix be
            of mound and breaker,   .
grain and droplet: how
        long can the freeze hold, the wind lie,
the free sand
keep the deep secret: turn: the gold
            grass will come
green in time, the dark stalks of rushes

32

will settle
    in the hollows, the ice bridge
    dissolving, yielding
will leave solid
bottom for summer fording: the black bushes
    will leaf,
hinder
the sea-bringing wind: turn turn

    here with these chances
taken, here to take these chances: land winds will
rise, feed
back the sands, humble the breakers: today's
    high unrelenting cry will relent:
the waves will lap with broken, separate,
    quiet sounds:
let the thaw that will come, come: the dissolved
    reorganizes
    to resilience.

SELF-PORTRAIT

In the desert a
clump of rocks
sang with hidden water:

    I broke in &
    water spilled:
    I planted trees:

wild animals from the hills
came at night
to tame water
and stood still:

    the air gathered
    hoverings of birds
    from
    drought's celestial trees:

grass sprouted
and spangled into seed:

    green reaches of
    streams went out:
    the rabbit that
    had visited,
    dwelled:

this was a dream.

PASSAGE

How, through what tube, mechanism,
unreal pass, does
    the past get ahead of us
to become today?

the dead are total mysteries, now:
their radiances,
    unwaxed by flesh, are put out:
disintegrations

occur, the black kingdom separates, loses
way, waters rush,
    gravel pours—
faces loosen, turn, and move:

that fact, that edge to turn around!
senselessly, then,
    celebrant with obscure
causes, unimaginable means, trickles

of possibility, the cull beads
catch centers, round out,
    luminescence stirs,
circulates through dark's depths

and there—all lost still lost—
the wells primed, the springs free,
    tomorrow emerges and
falls back shaped into today: endlessly.

PEAK

Everything begins at the tip-end, the dying-out,
    of mind:
the dazed eyes set and light
dissolves actual trees:

    the world beyond: tongueless,
unexampled
burns dimension out of shape,
opacity out of stone:

come: though the world ends and cannot
end,
    the apple falls sharp
to the heart starved with time.

ZONE

I spent the day
differentiating
and wound up
with nothing
whole to keep:

tree came apart from tree,
oak from maple, oak
from oak, leaf from leaf,
mesophyll cell
from cell
and toward dark
I got lost between
cytoplasm's grains
and vacuoles:

the next day began
otherwise: tree
became plant, plant
and animal became
life: life & rock,
matter: that
took up most of
the morning: after
noon, matter began
to pulse, shoot, to
vanish in and out of
energy and

energy's invisible
swirls confused, surpassed
me: from that edge

I turned back,

strict with limitation,
to my world's
bitter acorns
and sweet branch water.

MUSE

From the dark
fragmentations
    build me up
into a changed brilliant shape,

            realized order,
        mind singing again
new song, moving into the slow beat and

        disappearing beat
            of perfect resonance:

        how many
times must I be broken and reassembled!
    anguish of becoming,
        pain of moulting,
    descent! before the unending moment of vision:

how much disorder must I tolerate
    to find materials
        for the new house of my sight!

        arrange me
    into disorder
near the breaking of the pattern
but

        should disorder start to
tear, the breaking down of possible return,
    Oh rise gleaming in recall,

sing me again towering remade, born into a wider
        order, structures deepening,
            inching rootlike into the dark!

39

SITTING DOWN, LOOKING UP

A silver jet,
riding the top of tundra clouds,
comes over
maybe from Rio:
the aluminum sun shines
on it
as if it were a natural creature.

BELIEF
for JFK

1

drums gather and humble us beyond escape,
propound the single, falling fact :
time, suspended between memory and present,
hangs unmeasured, empty

2

erect,
disciplined by cadence into direction, the soldier
obeys the forms of rumor :
the riderless horse,
restive with the pressure of held flight,
tosses the hung bit,
worries the soldier's tameless arm —
sidling, prances the energy out

3

ahead, unalterable, the fact proceeds,
and the bit holds :
the fire-needle bites,
training the head on course

4

the light, determined rattle
of the caisson
breaking into sunlight
through the crystal black ribbons of trees !
the slack traces,
weightlessness at the shoulders of horses !

5

if we could break free
and run this knowledge out,
burst this energy of grief
through a hundred countrysides!
if bleak through the black night
we could outrun
this knowledge into a different morning!

6

belief, light as a drumrattle,
touches us and
lifts us into tears

SONG

Merging into place against a slope of trees,
I extended my arms and
took up the silence and spare leafage.
I lost my head first, the cervical meat
clumping off in rot,
baring the spinal heart to wind and ice

which work fast.
The environment lost no self-possession.
In spring, termites with tickling feet
aereated my veins.
A gall-nesting wren took my breath

flicking her wings, and
far into summer the termites found the heart.
No sign now shows the place,
all these seasons since,
but a hump of sod below the leaves
where chipmunks dig.

ORIENTALE

The pebble spoke and down
came the sun
   its plume
brushing through space as

over smooth sea-reaching stream
bent reed
   lets sodden leaf
arrow-ripples cut

and acorn husk wind-whirled
ran out and caught the sun
   in its burred cup
and said Look

to everyone standing on
edge of fern leaf watching
   the other edge
become imaginary as

waterbirds low-flying through
islands snake-long dark offshore
   Acorn husk got
no attention and even

the universe could sundering
hold no ear
   What somebody asked did
the pebble say

and sea colander washed
aland said Nothing
   nothing exists
and everybody watched to

see if fern leaf could
reappear with its lost edge
    and when
snow fell went in

MAYS LANDING

I sit in sun
light
on a white

yard-bench:
the sparse great
oaks

cower the county
buildings:
a bumblebee

works a head
of marigolds: the
jail back

there, keys rattle
a sheriff
by:

people stand about
in two's and
three's talking,

waiting for
court:
a drunk man

talks loud as
if sobering to
alarm:

an acorn whacks
through leaves and
cracks the ground!

SPHERE

In the dark original water,
amniotic infinity
closed
boundless in circularity:

    tame, heavy
water,
equilibriant,

any will forming to become—
consistency of motion
    arising—
annihilated
by its equal and opposite:

an even, complete extent:
    (there
an eden: how

foreign and far away
your death, rivulets
    trickling
through ripe bowels,

return to heavy water,
infinite multiplicity, in

the deepening, filtering
earthen womb
that bears you forever
    beyond

the amnion, O barrier!)

A warm unity, separable but
    entire,
you the nucleus
possessing that universe.

FIRST CAROLINA SAID-SONG

as told me by an aunt

In them days
    they won't hardly no way to know if
       somebody way off
       died
           till they'd be
           dead and buried

       and Uncle Jim

hitched up a team of mules to the wagon
and he cracked the whip over them
       and run them their dead-level best
the whole thirty miles to your great grandma's funeral
          down there in
          Green Sea County

          and there come up this
awfulest rainstorm
       you ever saw in your whole life
       and your grandpa
       was setting
       in a goatskin-bottom chair

and them mules a-running
and him sloshing round in that chairful of water
          till he got scalded
          he said
          and ev-
          ery

anch of skin come off his behind:

we got there just in time to see her buried
    in an oak grove up
    back of the field:
it's growed over with soapbushes and huckleberries now.

SECOND CAROLINA SAID-SONG

as told me by a patient, Ward 3-B,
Veterans Hospital, Fayetteville, August 1962

        I was walking down by the old
Santee
          River
          one evening, foredark
          fishing I reckon,

          when I come on this
swarm of
bees
          lit in the fork of a beech limb
          and they werz

          jest a swarming:

          it was too late to go home
          and too far
and brang a bee-gum

          so I waited around
          till the sun went
down,
most dark,

          and cut me off a pinebough,
          dipped it in the river
          and sprankled water
on'em: settled'em right down,
          good and solid,
about
          a bushel of

them:

　　when it got dark I first cut off
the fork branches and
then cut about four foot back toward
　　　　the trunk
and I
　　　throwed the limb over my shoulder
　　　and carried'em home.

DISCOVERER

If you must leave the shores of mind,
scramble down the walls
of dome-locked underwater caves
into the breathless, held

clarity of dark, where no waves break,
a grainy, colloidal grist
and quiet, carry a light: carry $A = \pi r^2$,
carry Kepler's equal areas in

equal times: as air line take Baudelaire's
L'Albatros: as depth markers
to call you back, fix the words of
the golden rule: feed the

night of your seeking with clusters
of ancient light:
remember the sacred sheaf, the rods of
civilization, the holy

bundle of elements: if to cast light
you must enter diffusion's ruin,
carry with you light to cast, to
gather darkness by: carry A is to B

as A plus B is to A: if to gather darkness
into light, evil into good,
you must leave the shores of mind,
remember us, return and rediscover us.

A SYMMETRY OF THOUGHT

is a mental object:
is to spirit
a rock of individual shape,
a flowerbed, pylon,
an arbor vitae
to cerebral loam:
is a moon in the mind,
water and land divided,
a crystal, precipitate,
separation, refinement,
a victory of being over void,
hazardous commitment,
broken eternity,
limited virtue;
coming into matter
spirit fallen
trades eternity
for temporal form:
is a symmetry of motion,
can always find its way
back to oblivion,
must move accommodating,
useful, relevant:
is, dead, a perfection;
here is its cage
to contemplate; here
time stops
and all its hollow bells
struck loud are
silenced in the never-ending sound.

HOLDING ON

The stone in my tire
sings by the strip of woods
but is
unheard by open fields:

surround me then with walls
before I risk
the outer sight —as, walled,
I'll soon long to.

UH, PHILOSOPHY

I understand
   reading the modern philosophers
that truth is so much a method
      it's perfectly all
right for me to believe whatever
   I like or if I like,

nothing:
   I do not know that I care to be set that free:
I am they say
      at liberty to be
provisional, to operate
   expediently, do not have to commit myself

to imperturbables, outright
   legislations, hardfast rules:
they say I can
      prefer my truths,
whatever
   suits my blood,

blends with my proclivities, my temperament:
   I suppose they mean I've had more experience than I can
ever read about, taking in
      as I do
possibly a hundred sensations per second, conscious
   and unconscious,

and making a vegetal at least
   synthesis
from them all, so that
      philosophy is
a pry pole, materialization,
   useful as a snowshovel when it snows;

something solid to knock people down with
     or back people up with:
I do not know that I care to be backed up in just that way:
          the philosophy gives clubs to
everyone, and I prefer disarmament:
     that is, I would rather relate

to the imperturbable objective
     than be the agent of
"possibly unsatisfactory eventualities":
          isn't anything plain true:
if I had something
     to conform to (without responsibility)

I wouldn't feel so hot and sticky:
     (but I must be moved by what I am moved by):
they do say, though, I must give some force to facts,
          must bend that way enough,
be in on the gist of "concrete observations,"
     must be pliant to the drift (roll with the knocks):

they say, too, I must halter my fancy
     mare
with these blinding limitations:
          I don't know that I can go along with that, either:
for though I've proved myself stupid by 33 years
     of getting nowhere,

I must nevertheless be given credit for the sense wherewith
     I decided never to set out:
what are facts if I can't line them up
          anyway I please
and have the freedom
     I refused I think in the beginning?

THE NUMBERS

                              are
                    consecutive:
          everything is real: no use

to worry: everything comes after everything,
safely held in count:

    experience, yes:
    remember that:
    selective memory: but the whole is difficult to
    recall, day by day:

    certain things are so clear:

think of the numbers, they proceed: there are five sparrows
at the feeder:
two are on the ground:
one is descending:

of those three on the ground
one is looking off,
toward or through the hedge, considering:

                         nevertheless, the count
                         is perfect:
                              942:

                    do not
              worry that anything
           is going to go wrong,
please:
turn to page 5: count two pages farther: count two pages
farther: count two pages farther:

                    where we are:
                    there is no use to worry:

58

grab the addendum:

today when the leaves fell it was
                    brilliant: shadows counted every one:
shadows broke against the limbs,
swept with several degrees of intensity across the grass,
moving
                    not as
                    the leaves
                    moved:
                    that was exciting:

the angles of descent (tho there is no use to worry) were not
predictable,
having to do with wind velocities and turns of leaf:

                    please turn to page 6:
                    all is explicable:

    here are the boxes: $4 \times 4 \times 4 \times 4 \times 4 \times 4 \times 4 \times 4$:
    how many? how many?

how many? how *many?*

many:

the numbers can set you free: square a pear:
                    pare a pair:
                    peel a peer:
                    a peer? appear
and seem:
                    be confident;
                    as you turn the numbers
                    veracity
                    links segment to segment: a sausage bliss!

        there is no reason:
        for concern:

falls wear the rock away
by a volume of noise: add it up:

think, think of the numbers, how they move!

appear and seem:
>the industrial buildings
>are as a shed of apples
>a truck has crushed through: musiked with
>bees!

there is no cause:
for concern: spell the numbers: gather them: the numbers
are consecutive:

EMPTY

Prison break!
  the single-idea bolt shot back!
    the grillwork
      of syllogism
  lake loose!
    the unyielding walls, square,
      sharp-cornered,
        fallen flat out
  to total openness!

          certain isolations:
          the diminished moon over cold
          sea:
          introduction of rocks
          and shrubs—the
          multiform land:

guilt diffused in limitless air:
punishment
    glittered dim among turning deep-sea schools:
      the unknown—pointless, vacant, blunt:

                    emptiness!

                    say everything again:
                    say everything over:

    cluck the words out of configuration,
    into configuration:
    remake:

          ramble:

    nothing has been established:
    the forms have not been placed:

the mixers are not ready:

the man will hear no answer:
he is not listening:
his heart knows shapeless music:
he is turned loose:
the prison is broken

UNBROKEN

Evening falls: earth
  divides:
    insects waken
  as
birds fly to roost:

out there, nothing
  happens:
    everything is
  the
same.

FALL

Summer gauds,
crickets
sing:
the cool-snap
quavers their song
beyond
meanings they intend.

THE WIND COMING DOWN FROM

summit and blue air
said I am sorry for you
and lifting past
   said you
are mere dust which I
   as you see control

yet nevertheless are
   instrument of miracle

and rose
   out of earshot but
returning in a slow loop
   said while
I am always just this bunch of
   compensating laws
pushed, pushing
   not air or motion
but the motion of air

I coughed
   and the wind said
Ezra will live
to see your last
   sun come up again

I turned (as I will) to weeds and
the wind went off
   carving
monuments through a field of stone
   monuments whose shape
wind cannot arrest but
taking hold on

changes

while Ezra
    listens from terraces of mind
wind cannot reach or
weedroots of my low-feeding shiver

INTERVAL

Coming to a pinywoods
     where a stream darted across the path
like a squirrel or frightened blacksnake
I sat down on a sunny hillock
     and leaned back against a pine
and picked up some dry pineneedle bundles from the ground
and tore each bundle apart a needle at a time
     It was not Coulter's pine
     for *coulteri* is funnier-looking
     and not Monterrey either
and I thought God must have had Linnaeus in mind
orders of trees correspond so well between them
and I dropped to sleep wondering what design God
had meant the human mind to fit
     and looked up and saw a great bird
warming in the sun high on a pine limb
tearing from his breast golden feathers
     softer than new gold that
     dropped to the wind one or two
     gently and touched my face
I picked one up and it said
     The world is bright after rain
for rain washes death out of the land and hides it far
beneath the soil and it returns again cleansed with life
     and so all is a circle
and nothing is separable
The mind a loosely held bundle of sensibilities
     falls apart
     and rushes over the earth
     re-forming in many places
Look at this pine from which you are
almost indistinguishable it is also sensible

and cries out when it is felled
and so I said are trees blind and is the earth black to them
Oh if trees are blind
I do not want to be a tree
A wind rising of *one in time* blowing the feather away
forsaken I woke
and the golden bird had flown away and the sun
had moved the shadows over me so I rose and walked on

WAY TO GO

West light flat on trees:
   bird flying
      deep out in blue glass:
   uncertain wind
stirring the leaves: this is
   the world we have:
      take it